tea with friends

ELIZABETH KNIGHT
Illustrated by Carolyn Bucha

STOREY
BOOKS

Schoolhouse Road
Pownal, Vermont 05261

*The mission of Storey Communications is to serve our customers
by publishing practical information that encourages personal independence
in harmony with the environment.*

Edited by Deborah Balmuth and Robin Catalano
Design and production by Carol Jessop, Black Trout Design

Tea and food pairing suggestions courtesy of The British Tea Council, Ltd. Hot tea concentrate recipe courtesy of The Lipton Co. Iced tea recipe courtesy of The Tea Council of the U.S.A.

Printed in Mexico by R.R. Donnelley
10 9 8 7 6 5 4 3 2

Library of Congress Cataloging-in-Publication Data

Knight, Elizabeth D., 1948–
    Tea with Friends/Elizabeth D. Knight; illustrations by Carolyn Bucha.
        p.   cm.
    ISBN 1-58017-050-1 (alk. paper)
    1. Afternoon teas. 2. Tea. 3. Holiday cookery. I. Title.
TX736.K55   1998
641.5'3--dc21

98-11986
CIP

dedication:

In memory of

Eleanor Nicholson

Knight and with

thanks to Eileen

Marshall Murphy.

Contents

taking tea

Intimate, practical, and unique, a tea party is the ultimate form of hospitality. No longer bound by stuffy traditions, today's teas lend themselves to a host of formal and informal celebrations such as bridal and baby showers, picnics, birthday parties, recitals, reunions, and business meetings. Teas — be they midmorning elevenses, traditional afternoon, or high tea suppers — always lift the spirits! So isn't it time you took a break from your overbooked life to share the cup that cheers with family and friends?

Two Leaves and a Bud

Water is the world's most popular and least expensive beverage, but tea is second. All the world's tea — more than three thousand varieties — comes from just one plant, the *Camellia sinensis,* an evergreen bush with dark green, leathery leaves, and from its hybrids. Native to Asia, tea is grown in hot, humid regions and varies in flavor according to soil, altitude, and climate. The delicate first two leaves and bud are prized over the less flavorful mature leaves. Processing methods determine whether the tea you drink is black, oolong, or green.

Black Tea is fully fermented. Freshly plucked green leaves are spread out to wither and then twisted so the natural enzymes are released and oxidize. Finally, the leaves are dried to become the familiar black leaf noted for its rich, full-bodied brew.

Green Tea, the brew's oldest form, is unfermented and merely steamed, rolled, and dried. Chinese varieties are more mellow than "grassy" Japanese teas.

Oolong Tea (Chinese for "black dragon") is semifermented. The flavor is a "compromise" between black and green teas.

Blended Teas are combinations of different teas which ensure a quality product under changing growing conditions. Flowers, fruit, herbs, or spices may be part of the mix.

Herbal Teas, which are made with herbs, flowers, fruit, roots, berries, bark, or the leaves of any plant other than *Camellia sinensis,* are not true tea. Technically, such caffeine-free drinks are called infusions or tisanes. Folk wisdom values these concoctions for their soothing and healing properties.

"drinking a daily cup of tea will surely starve the apothec'ry."
— Chinese proverb

all tea types are high in vitamins A, B, C, and E; minerals such as fluoride, iron, manganese, magnesium, zinc, and potassium; and antioxidants. Tea also contains substances that lower blood pressure and cholesterol and stabilize blood sugar. A cup of black tea, brewed for 5 minutes, contains just one-third the caffeine of a cup of non-espresso, black coffee. How much tea must you drink to reap all these benefits? Experts recommend two cups in the morning and another two at night, of any type tea.

A GUIDE TO TEAS

	place of origin	name	description
BLACK TEAS	Africa	Kenya	Rich, robust
	Ceylon (say-LAHN)	Dimbula (dim-BOO-lah) Nuwara Eliya (NEW-wah-RAHL-lay-yah)	Smooth, refreshing Light, with woody scent
	China	Keemun	Full-flavored, with delicate orchidlike scent
	China	Lapsang Souchong (SUE-chong)	Distinctive smoky, complex flavor
	China	Yunnan (YOU-nan)	Potent, peppery
	India	Assam (ah-SAHM)	Strong, malty
	India	Darjeeling (dar-JEE-LING)	Delicate, lingering flavor, lovely amber color
	India	Nilgiri (neal-GEAR-E)	Used to make Chai Masala, it makes a fragrant cuppa on its own
GREEN TEAS	China	Dragon Well	Sweet, smooth, nutlike flavor
	China	Gunpowder	Pungent, slightly bitter
	China	Jasmine	Jasmine scented
	Japan	Gyokuro (Guy-oh-KOOR-oh)	Mild, slightly sweet
OOLONG	China	Iron Goddess of Mercy	Copper-colored, astringent, digestive aid
	Taiwan	Formosa Oolong	Peachy, peppery
BLENDED/SPECIALTY TEAS		Earl Grey	Chinese black and Indian Darjeeling teas scented with bergamot oil; aromatic, assertive
		English Breakfast	Black teas from India and Ceylon, full-bodied
		Irish Breakfast	Mostly Assam, hearty, invigorating
		Russian Caravan	Strong black teas with a touch of Lapsang Souchong

brewing time	serving suggestions	complementary foods
2–4 minutes	Take plain, or with milk and lemon	Strong flavors, both savory and sweet
3–5 minutes	Serve with/without milk, lemon, or ice	Cucumber or tomato sandwiches, lemon pastries
5 minutes	Serve with/without milk, sugar, or lemon	White meat, fish, or Chinese foods
3–5 minutes	Serve with/without milk, sugar	Chicken, smoked salmon, and lemony desserts
3–5 minutes	Take with/without milk	Highly seasoned foods
3–5 minutes	Milk enhances flavor	
3–5 minutes	Serve with/without milk or lemon	Egg or cream cheese sandwiches and creamy desserts
3–5 minutes		
1–3 minutes with water just below boiling	Traditionally, green teas are drunk without milk, lemon, or sugar; Dragon Well is a good hot-weather thirst quencher	
1–3 minutes with water just below boiling	See above	
1–3 minutes with water just below boiling	See above	Strongly flavored foods
1–3 minutes with water just below boiling	See above	
1–7 minutes	Best taken neat, without milk, lemon, or sugar	
1–7 minutes	See above	Chicken, cheese, seafood, fresh fruit
3–5 minutes	Take with/without milk	Strong, savory dishes and rich desserts
3–5 minutes	Drink with/without milk or lemon any time of day; good iced	
3–5 minutes	Best with milk	
3–5 minutes	Take with/without milk or lemon; good iced; ideal afternoon or evening tea	

to own a porcelain teacup in the eighteenth century was to enjoy high social standing. Proud owners had their portraits painted holding a favorite cup. Guests toted to parties their own cups in special padded cases. Handles didn't exist until about one hundred years ago. Before that, tea was drunk, Chinese-style, from a bowl whose saucer served as a lid to keep the beverage hot. Tea was poured into the saucer to cool before drinking — hence, a "dish of tea."

MORE THAN JUST A CUPPA: TEA THE MEAL

Afternoon tea, or low tea, was "invented" by Anna Maria, the seventh Duchess of Bedford (1783–1857), one of Queen Victoria's ladies-in-waiting. In her day, the upper crust ate a huge breakfast, little lunch, and a very late dinner. Every afternoon, at about five o'clock, the duchess experienced "a sinking feeling." One afternoon she instructed her servants to serve tea and little cakes in her boudoir. The experience was so delightful that Anna Maria repeated it every afternoon thereafter. Adopted by the queen, the duchess' secret snack became an elaborate and much loved domestic ceremony. Today we enjoy several types of English-style tea parties.

Afternoon tea, served between three and five o'clock, is always an elegant snack rather than a meal. The menu usually includes several kinds of finger sandwiches, scones, assorted pastries (tiny cookies, tarts, petits fours), loaf or fruit cake, and possibly a more elaborate layer cake or trifle as a finale. Traditionally, this dainty fare was presented on a low side table, with lacy linens and the best china and silver, beside a comfortable armchair in the drawing room. The Victorian hostess made and poured the tea while gentleman guests handed round the cups and passed the elegant edibles.

Cream tea, sometimes called light tea, consists of hot scones, jam, and clotted cream.

Elevenses, similar to our mid-morning coffee break, is tea with a simple snack.

High tea, served from six o'clock on, is a hearty, homey, "sit-down" meal that began as a working-class supper during the Industrial Revolution. Workers home from the factories and fields were served savory or meat dishes, bread and cheese, and homemade cake or pie at the dining table.

PLANNING YOUR TEA PARTY

The Guest List. Choose people of any age with whom you feel comfortable. If this is your first tea party, start small — no more than three or four guests. Invite at least one person you'd like to know better.

Timing. Any time is teatime. Sunday afternoon is ideal because it allows ample time for preparations, dinner plans are not affected, and everybody goes home early.

The Invitation. Allow two weeks' notice. You may telephone, but it's more festive for your guests to receive a written invitation. Make the message simple — include the date, time, address, telephone number, and the phrase "Regrets Only by *(date)*," and sign your name at the bottom.

The Perfect Setting. Taking tea is an intimate experience. Furniture should be arranged in comfortable, conversational groupings. Afternoon tea lends itself to a living room or library.

High tea is best laid in the dining room or buffet-style from a living room sideboard. Elevenses and cream tea suit the kitchen, family room, or den. Really casual parties could take place on a porch, under a backyard tree, at the beach, or even tucked in bed!

What to Serve. "Something savory, something sweet, and all things delicious" is a good guide, and your menu should reflect the season. Iced, fruity, and flowery teas are refreshing; strongly flavored and spiced teas are warming. You might offer a choice of tea as well as an herbal infusion. The earlier in the day that tea is served, the lighter the fare. Arrange food in progression from savory to sweet. It is customary to serve a second beverage in addition to tea at a large reception.

Consult the superabundance of afternoon-tea cookbooks or cookbooks from the 1920s to the 1950s for specific menus and recipes.

Sandwich Savvy. Use firm, thinly sliced bread — white, whole wheat, oatmeal, pumpernickel, sourdough, and rye are easy to find. Spread slices to the edge with softened unsalted butter or a mix of half butter, half cream cheese to protect bread from soggy fillings. Arrange sandwiches, one layer deep, on cookie sheets; cover with waxed paper and a well-wrung, damp dish towel; and refrigerate until time to serve. Just before serving, trim crusts with a serrated knife and cut into fingers or triangles. Two pieces of bread with filling make four tiny sandwiches. Figure three to five assorted sandwiches per person.

Scottish kings were crowned on the Stone of Scone (Destiny), which legend says was Jacob's pillow. (In southern England these little stone-shaped biscuits are pronounced to rhyme with lawn, but farther north scone rhymes with loan.) At a "veddy" proper tea you'd split your scone in half horizontally, spread it with only one bite's worth of jam, and top with a dollop of clotted cream. True clotted cream is unavailable in the United States, but upscale markets stock Somerdale or English Double Devon Cream. Other scrumptious substitutes are crème fraîche, mascarpone, and whipped cream.

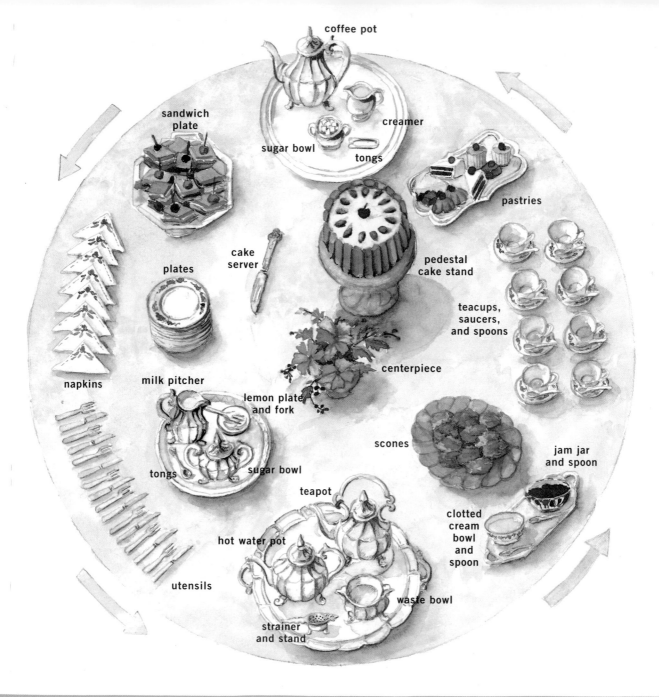

coffee pot

sandwich plate

sugar bowl

creamer

tongs

pastries

cake server

plates

pedestal cake stand

teacups, saucers, and spoons

napkins

milk pitcher

lemon plate and fork

centerpiece

tongs

sugar bowl

scones

jam jar and spoon

teapot

hot water pot

clotted cream bowl and spoon

utensils

waste bowl

strainer and stand

SET TO A TEA: THE TEA TABLE

tea may be served from a dining table, coffee table, sideboard, cart, or tray. Cloth napkins are a must. A variety of serving pieces in different heights, shapes, and materials will add visual interest to your table. Don't fret if you haven't got a matched tea set. Assemble these elements, mixing patterns and materials, to create a unique and stylish setting:

Centerpiece. Keep fresh flowers or plants small and below eye level or airy and "see-through." Do not light candles unless it is dark enough to need them.

Clotted cream bowl and spoon; jam jar and spoon; butter dish and knife. Shallow glass or ceramic bowls, compote dishes, and even saucer champagne glasses add sparkle.

Cozy. This colorful padded or quilted fabric covers your teapot to keep the contents piping hot.

Creamer or pitcher. Used for serving milk, this piece usually matches the sugar bowl.

Lemon plate and fork. Any small plate may be used; place a two-pronged fork atop thinly sliced lemon.

Pedestal cake stand. Line the surface with a napkin or doily.

Sandwich plate. This rectangular or square plate may also be used for sweets.

Strainer and stand. Use these to remove loose tea and to prevent drips from staining the tablecloth.

Sugar bowl. The lid is removed and a spoon, tongs, or sugar shell is placed inside. If serving honey, use a small pitcher.

Teacups, saucers, and plates. Pieces need not match as long as they complement each other and share common colors.

Teapot. Silver is the queen of metals, but a ceramic pot, pottery, or bone china holds heat better. Use a pot large enough to pour each guest one cup of tea, but not too heavy to lift easily. Add a second, smaller pot filled with hot water for diluting strong tea.

Tiered server. Stack, from the top down, with scones, sandwiches, and pastries.

Tray. Choose one to reflect the formal or informal nature of your party. The tray should be big enough to hold "inedible necessities."

Utensils. Anticipate serving needs according to your menu.

Waste bowl. This is any small, widemouthed bowl in which the cold tea dregs may be dumped.

TEA FOR A CROWD

The practical way to make hot tea for a crowd is to make a concentrate ahead of time. Another option is to invest in an electric tea maker. Follow the directions to the right for brewing a perfect cup, but use the following proportions.

Use 2 tablespoons of tea concentrate for each cup of hot tea. Fill each cup with hot water and add milk, sugar, or lemon, if desired.

25 servings
1 quart boiling water
½ cup loose tea or 25 regular cup-size tea bags

50 servings
2 quarts boiling water
1 cup loose tea or 50 regular cup-size tea bags

100 servings
1 gallon boiling water
2 cups loose tea or 100 regular cup-size tea bags

TEACRAFT: HOW TO MAKE A PERFECT CUPPA

1. Use freshly drawn cold water. For full tea flavor, let the tap run for a few minutes so that the water will be filled with oxygen, or use bottled water or springwater; avoid flavorless distilled water.

2. "Hot" the pot. To preheat the teapot, rinse with nearly boiling water, swirl the water about, and discard through the spout. If you skip this step, the water temperature will drop on contact with the cold pot and the tea's flavor will suffer.

3. Measure 1 teaspoon loose tea per cup (or 1 teabag for each 2 cups of tea). Add "one for the pot" if you like strong tea. Deposit loose tea in a pot, fabric tea sock, paper filter, or infusing basket. Wire mesh balls cramp leaves. If you use one, fill no more than halfway so water can circulate.

4. Bring the water to a full rolling boil. When the steam shoots straight up, bring the pot to the kettle and pour water over the leaves/bags. Dunking a tea bag in water makes mediocre tea. Water that is not hot enough or overboiled results in flat-tasting tea. Cover the pot with the lid and immediately pop on a quilted cozy or pot holder to hold heat.

5. Brew by the clock. Never attempt to judge tea strength by color. The larger the leaf, the longer the brewing time. Steep black teas 3 to 5 minutes; any longer and the tea might be bitter. Herbal teas may take more time. Green and oolong teas are more delicate than black. You don't want to cook the leaves, so brew 1 to 3 minutes with water that has not quite boiled.

6. Strain. Remove the leaves/bags to prevent further steeping. Stir the tea and serve immediately, or cover with a cozy to keep hot. The third cup will taste as good as the first!

Terrific Iced Tea

To make a 2-quart pitcherful of iced tea, bring one quart of freshly drawn cold water to a full rolling boil in a saucepan. Remove from heat and immediately add fifteen tea bags or ⅓ cup loose tea. Stir, then cover and steep five minutes. Stir again and strain into a pitcher holding an additional quart of freshly drawn cold water. Freeze fruit juice, lemonade, or mint syrup (equal parts water and sugar, freshly chopped mint to taste; boil 5 minutes) into ice cube trays for a taste treat.

Teacraft: How to Store Tea

Buy the best-quality tea you can afford, often and in small amounts. Tea loses flavor when exposed to light, air, and moisture. Store in a sealed tin or airtight ceramic container. Don't store tea in the refrigerator or with strong-flavored foods. Taylor's of Harrogate, a British tea company founded in 1886, suggests that tainted tea may be revived by spreading leaves on a sheet of paper to air for a few hours. Black tea may be kept successfully for more than a year; oolong, up to a year. Enjoy green as soon as possible after purchase.

Selecting and Using a Teapot

Silver and stainless steel are the only metals that won't "taint" tea flavor. Aluminum and enamel are fine for tea *kettles*, however. Ceramic pots are best for holding heat. Check for a smooth, crack-free glaze inside and out. Down-turned spouts drip less. Look for lids with a lug lock and those that have a small hole for increased air flow. Use your teapot solely for brewing tea; it can absorb the flavor of other beverages. Rinse, rather than wash, pots — you don't want future servings to taste soapy. Remove stains with a solution of hot water and 4 tablespoons baking soda.

Tea with a Twist

According to Mr. Twining, head of the House of Twining, roses have a passion for cold tea leaves and African violets and ferns for cold tea, so recycle leftover leaves and liquor and "water" these plants with a brew. Here are some other ways to use this versatile beverage: Soothe sunburns, relieve puffy eyes, and revive sweaty feet with cold tea compresses; tea spiked with lemon juice makes an excellent oily skin astringent; dye dingy lingerie a lovely champagne color with a medium-strong solution of cooled black tea; remove fish or onion odors by scrubbing the pan in which they were cooked with damp tea leaves.

Shall I Be Mum?

this question is asked to determine who shall have the honor of pouring the tea. The host or hostess pours the first cup for each guest at an informal party.

"Mum" asks each guest the following questions:

"Do you take your tea strong or weak?" If weak, fill cup only three-quarters full so guests may dilute with water.

"Plain, milk, sugar, or lemon?" Never combine milk with lemon because acid curdles milk. When lemon is desired, place the slice in the bottom of the cup, then top with tea.

january

HOGMANAY HIGH TEA

January got its name from the Roman god Janus, who opened the door to the new year. Sacrifices were customarily offered to secure his blessing before important undertakings, and especially on New Year's Day. Since the ancients believed that the year would end as it had begun, customs such as paying debts, mending quarrels, and wearing new clothes were observed in hopes that the coming year would bring prosperity and peace. Today, we still host parties, dress up, and eat special foods to secure a year's worth of luck.

In Scotland, Hogmanay (HOG-muh-nay), or New Year, was traditionally a bigger celebration than Christmas. At midnight, folks fortified with a bottle of whiskey, oatcakes, and a piece of coal set off to "first-foot" their neighbors, sharing the "necessities of life" for luck. Highlanders considered a dark-haired man the luckiest first-footer to cross the threshold.

"Be kind and courteous to all, even to the stranger from afar. If he say to thee that he thirsteth, give unto him a cup of tea."
— Confucius

January is national hot tea month—tea's popularity is soaring.

I've made a resolution hearty
to start the year off right with a High Tea Party!
Join me for a New Year's Day Open House
Thursday, January 1

Beverages

Lapsang Souchong tea, perhaps with a wee dram of whiskey

Wassail punch

Savories

Baked ham

Hoppin' John rice and black-eyed peas casserole

Spinach salad

Sandwiches

Smoked salmon with dill and lemon crème fraîche, on pumpernickel

Cucumber and watercress on white bread

Cream cheese with finely chopped crystallized ginger, on date-nut bread

Sweets

Scottish Scones (see recipe)

Shortbread petticoats, tips dipped in chocolate

Black bun fruitcake

SETTING THE SCENE

If your Christmas tree is still up, you won't need much else in the way of decorations. No tree? How about topiaries or pots of heather on either side of a mantel? Wind greenery — symbol of a fresh start — and tartan ribbon around door and windows. Gather masses of white pillar candles trimmed with narrow tartan ribbon to cast a cheery glow. Store candles in the freezer for several hours to diminish drips. Never place candles near flammable materials or a draft.

For a centerpiece, use a tartan runner and a large footed platter piled with pomegranates, symbol of plenty. Tuck greenery, heather, and miniature red gerbera daisies in the gaps between fruit. Cut a few open to display the ruby seeds. Arrange colorful party crackers (popular party favors from the British Isles) in a basket lined with a tartan napkin.

For music, the skirl o' bagpipes, spirited reels, or stirring ballads will get everyone in a Brigadoon mood. Look for tapes and CDs in the World Music section at larger record stores.

SCOTTISH SCONES

1¾ C unbleached all-purpose flour	Preheat oven to 400° F. Combine first five ingredients in the bowl of a food processor. Blend in butter until mixture looks like fine crumbs. Do not overmix.
4 Tbsp sugar	
2½ tsp baking powder	In large bowl, beat 1 egg and add flour mixture. Stir in raisins and enough of the cream so that dough forms a ball. Turn dough onto lightly floured surface and knead about 10 times. Roll out to ½-inch thickness.
½ tsp salt	
1½ tsp minced fresh lemon thyme	
⅓ C butter	Beat the other egg. Cut dough into circles with a biscuit cutter, place circles on an ungreased cookie sheet, and brush with beaten egg. Bake for 10 to 12 minutes, or until golden brown. Cool on wire rack or serve warm.
2 eggs	
½ C raisins, chopped	
1–6 Tbsp light cream	

10–12 scones

Canny Scots used to read breakfast tea leaves to "predict" how the day would go. Guests might like to see what the future holds for them on this first day of the new year. Here's how to do it:

Make a pot of strong black tea with loose leaves. Without using a strainer, pour a generous amount into a cup with a plain interior. Sip slowly and either make a wish or think about a specific topic. When there's about a tablespoon of tea left in your cup, swirl it around three times, counterclockwise, using your left hand. Turn the cup upside down onto the saucer, handle pointing toward you, and wait 3 minutes. Take up the cup in both hands and turn it over.

The teacup handle is the present, leaves on the cup bottom refer to the distant future, and those near the rim concern the immediate future. If the leaves are dispersed, forming no distinct pattern, your thoughts are too scattered to read the leaves successfully.

PATTERN ⟶	MEANING
AIRPLANE ⟶	PROMOTION
ANCHOR ⟶	SUCCESS OR VOYAGE
BIRD, CAT, TREE ⟶	GOOD LUCK
BOOK ⟶	REVELATION
CIRCLE ⟶	GOOD LUCK,
	UNLESS CIRCLE IS BROKEN
CROSS, SNAKE ⟶	TROUBLE
DAGGER ⟶	DANGER
DOG ⟶	FAITHFUL FRIEND
FISH ⟶	MONEY
HEART ⟶	LOVE AFFAIR
HOUSE ⟶	SUCCESS
LADDER ⟶	OPPORTUNITY
TRIANGLE ⟶	INHERITANCE
WINGS ⟶	IMPORTANT MESSAGE

"MY CUP RUNNETH OVER WITH LOVE"

— Jones/Schmidt, "My Cup Runneth Over"

february

NOT-FOR-LOVERS-ONLY DESSERT TEA

Our Valentine's Day is an adaptation of a holiday celebrated by ancient Romans in honor of Pan and Juno. On February 14, maidens wrote their names on slips of paper and placed them in a jar. Single men dipped their hands into the jar to find the name of a sweetheart. There were two St. Valentines martyred on that date in third-century Rome. One, a priest, was killed for performing marriages, a practice the emperor disliked because married men were reluctant to go to war. The other Valentine, jailed for aiding Christians, pricked a violet's heart-shaped leaves with the message "Remember your Valentine" and a dove delivered the notes to the saint's loved ones. Today, doves decorate valentines, heart-shaped symbols of giving the essence of self.

About two weeks before Valentine's Day, send out invitations asking friends to a pre–Valentine's Day card-making party.

My cup would runneth over
if you'd join me for a love-ly pot of tea
and Valentine-making active-i-teas
Sunday, February 7

In the Middle Ages people noticed that partridges, blackbirds, and thrushes mated in February. Romantics decided that "each bird doth choose a mate, this day St. Valentine's." Doves — messengers of the gods and sacred to Venus — came to be associated with true love because they mate for life.

SETTING THE SCENE

february can be very gray and gloomy, but pots of flowering plants will brighten things up considerably. Stick to one type and color — an assembly of red parrot tulips or pink cyclamen, for instance. Pop plastic containers into clay pots stenciled with hearts (use acrylic craft paint), or swaddle them in tissue paper gathered with wired ribbon for perfect bows. Glue bamboo skewers to valentine backs and tuck around blossoms.

For a centerpiece, shop the discount or pet stores for an inexpensive birdcage. Gild it with gold spray paint and make a lush, long-tailed bow for the top with red and white tulle (netting). Wire an artificial dove (from a floral-supply or crafts store) onto the bow knot and another onto the bird swing. Fill the cage with a potted plant or scatter about construction paper hearts.

For music, Ella Fitzgerald singing the *Cole Porter Songbook* offers witty inspiration and Frank Sinatra's *Only the Lonely* album is a real tearjerker.

PEPPERMINT ANGEL FOOD CAKE

1 C cake flour	Preheat oven to 350° F. Use nonstick baking paper to line the base of an ungreased angel food cake pan.
2 Tbsp cornstarch	
¾ C granulated sugar	Sift together flour, cornstarch, and 1 tablespoon of the sugar.
5 large egg whites	Beat egg whites until stiff. Using a whisk, gradually add the rest of the sugar. Continue to whisk the mixture until very thick.
½ tsp vanilla extract	
1 Tbsp finely chopped fresh peppermint	Fold in flour mixture, vanilla, and mint. Turn into the pan and bake 35 to 40 minutes.
	Invert the cake, still in pan, over a tray of ice cubes to cool. Do not unmold until cold.

6 servings

CREATING VALENTINES

assemble all the makings on a sturdy table: construction and tissue paper, scissors, glue, paper doilies, stacks of magazines (a rich source of images, especially perfume and chocolate ads, for those who don't draw), crayons, markers, cookie cutters (to trace around), glitter, sequins, rubber stamps, stickers, stapler, ruler, yarn, ribbons, and lace. Invite guests to make cards for *anyone* who has given them the gift of love. Someone might want to thank a high school English teacher for sharing the love of books; another might want to honor a pet for the gift of unconditional love. You could also contact a local hospital or nursing home and make valentines for those who receive no visitors.

Consult a quotations dictionary for lover-ly sentiments such as this one from Shakespeare: "For thy sweet love rememb'red such wealth brings/That then I scorn to change my state with kings." Tuck a sprig of rosemary — for remembrance — through a heart inscribed with the quote, and send it to a long-lost love.

march

ST. PATRICK'S DAY CEILI TEA

March 17 is celebrated by Irish people all over the world as St. Patrick's feast day.

The man behind the holiday, said to be responsible for converting the Irish to Christianity by illustrating the mystery of the Trinity with a shamrock, was actually Scottish! Patricus was what Maewyn Succat called himself in his collected writings. Perhaps the most famous legend about St. Patrick is that he drove all the snakes out of Ireland by banging a drum while standing knee-deep in shamrocks. As St. Patrick lay dying on this day in 464 A.D., the bishop urged friends to celebrate his "comfortable exit" and lighten their heavy hearts with a small drop of whiskey.

Country people still celebrate St. Patrick's Day by drinking Pota Padraig. In some towns, bagpipers and step dancers still parade down the main street. Invite friends to a ceili (KAY-lee), a traditional Celtic form of entertainment from the days when people made their own fun.

Wearing and eating something green on St. Paddy's Day will bring good luck.

In honor of St. Patrick's Day, join me for a cup of tay!
Please prepare to toast the auld sod with an Irish
story, song, or poem.
Tuesday, March 17

Beverages
Irish breakfast tea

Irish coffee

Savories
Potato and leek tartlets

Sandwiches
Egg-watercress salad
on multigrain bread

Smoked salmon and cream
cheese pinwheels
on white bread

Avocado spread with bacon bits,
on whole wheat

Sweets
Irish Soda Bread (see recipe)

Green tea ice cream

Gingerbread with clotted cream

Shamrock-shaped sugar cookies

SETTING THE SCENE

after a long, dark winter, a glimpse of green is very welcome. Pots or flats of live shamrocks may be purchased inexpensively from most florists. Float tea light or small votive candles in bowls of water with moss islands. Hang a banner on your door reading *Cead Mile Failte:* 100,000 Welcomes.

For a centerpiece, if you're fortunate enough to own "cottage-ware" — tea things that look like a rustic thatched cottage — give them center stage and ring with potted shamrocks. If not, create a centerpiece by turning a green cardboard top hat (available from a party/crafts store) upside down and stuffing it three-quarters full with crumpled newspaper. Fill the top third with scrubbed potatoes and tuck in a shamrock plant. Nestle a large potato labeled BLARNEY STONE next to the hat. If you have a leprechaun figurine, he can perch on the hat or the Blarney Stone.

For music, there are as many kinds of Irish music as there are shades of green — infectious foot-stomping reels and jigs; haunting harp tunes; and music of the Bodhran drum, fiddle, and tin whistle.

IRISH SODA BREAD

4 C all-purpose flour, plus 1 Tbsp for dusting	Heat oven to 350° F. Grease 9-inch round cast-iron skillet or baking pan.
2 tsp baking powder	In a large bowl combine 4 cups flour, baking powder, baking soda, salt, sugar, raisins, and caraway seeds.
1 tsp baking soda	Blend eggs, buttermilk, and sour cream in a small bowl. Stir into flour mixture until flour is just moistened.
¾ tsp salt	
½ C sugar	Knead dough in bowl, about 10 strokes. (Dough will be very sticky.) Shape into a ball and place in skillet.
3 C dark seedless raisins	Make 4-inch by ¾-inch deep cut across top of dough. Sprinkle with remaining flour.
1 Tbsp caraway seeds	
2 eggs, lightly beaten	Bake 65–75 minutes, or until toothpick inserted in center comes out clean. Cool in skillet 10 minutes.
1¼ C buttermilk	Turn out bread onto wire rack to cool completely.
1 C sour cream	**20 slices**

SINGING AND DANCING

a *ceili* is traditionally an evening of Irish dancing and singing. If you don't have room to kick up your heels, invite guests to celebrate Ireland's rich cultural heritage in story and song. Collect sheet music with favorites like "When Irish Eyes are Smiling" and "How Are Things in Glocca Morra?" Before the party, ask someone with a strong voice to lead a sing-along — sort of like Christmas caroling in March.

It is remarkable that such a small island contributed so much literary genius — the satirist Jonathan Swift; poet William Butler Yeats; playwrights Shaw, Wilde, and O'Casey. Guests might recite a poem, read a part in a play, or tell a tall tale. Anyone needing inspiration can kiss the Blarney stone!

When Queen Elizabeth I asked the Irish Cormac MacDermot MacCarthy — Lord Blarney — to swear allegiance to the English crown, he diverted her with dozens of glib and irrelevant promises. The exasperated queen declared that she didn't believe a word he said. Today, those seeking the gift of gab must climb to the top of Blarney Castle in County Cork, Ireland, lie down backward and lean over to kiss the Blarney stone.

april

APRIL FOOL'S DAY MADCAP TEA

april has been called the cruelest month, her fickle nature making fools of mankind. But perhaps man contributed to the confusion. According to the Alban calendar, April had thirty-six days, and New Year's frequently fell on the first. But in 1564, the Gregorian calendar stipulated that New Year's Day would now be celebrated on January first. Many people were confused about New Year's changing date and the mix-up provided an ideal opportunity to play practical jokes on the unsuspecting.

In the British Isles gullible people were sent on fool's errands to buy a left-handed hammer or a pint of pigeon's milk. Scottish simpletons, called April Gawks, were encouraged to "hunt the (nonexistent) gawk another mile." European settlers imported this funny business to America, where jesters must complete their tomfoolery before noon because the late trickster is the ultimate April Fool. You might celebrate the day with a madcap tea.

In olden days a tea made with ground ivy was drunk on April 8 as a protection against spring fever.

"Mirth is the sugar of life."
Just for fun, join me for a madcap tea!
Wednesday, April 1

MENU

Fool your guests into eating their vegetables with a chocolate zucchini cake.

Beverages

Formosa oolong tea

Champagne or sparkling cider

Savories

Sweet/spiced cocktail nuts

Sandwiches

Cranberry-orange chicken salad on multigrain bread

Melba toast topped with goat cheese and diced bell pepper spread

Wafer-thin radish rounds with sweet butter on white bread

Sweets

Ladyfingers filled with vanilla pastry cream and sliced strawberries

Chocolate Zucchini Cake (see recipe)

Lemon tea cookies

SETTING THE SCENE

take courage from Clarice Ciff's boldly colored "Bizarre" teaware from the 1930s and combine colors and patterns in a whimsical way. Rustle up a different color or style cup and saucer for each person. Today is the day to use that funny fish-shaped teapot. Recycle a chipped teapot as a planter to hold sweet peas, April's flower. Instead of a tablecloth, dress the table with a shawl or bright chenille bedspread. Tether a balloon bouquet to a big-brimmed hat and mount it on your front door.

For a centerpiece, gather a lighthearted collection of clown dolls or jester figurines to prance down the middle of the table.

For music, something sprightly like Mozart, P.D.Q. Bach, or frothy Strauss waltzes should put everyone in a playful mood.

CHOCOLATE ZUCCHINI CAKE

4 oz unsweetened chocolate	Preheat oven to 350° F.
$\frac{1}{2}$ C vegetable oil	Melt chocolate and combine with oil in a small bowl.
$\frac{1}{2}$ C softened butter	In a large bowl, cream together butter and sugar
2 C sugar	until light and fluffy. Add vanilla and eggs and beat
1 Tbsp vanilla extract	well. Stir in chocolate mixture until well mixed.
3 eggs, beaten	Sift dry ingredients into the batter and add
2 C flour, sifted	buttermilk. Stir until smooth. Mix zucchini and
$\frac{1}{3}$ C cocoa	nuts into batter.
2 tsp baking soda	Pour batter into 9-inch by 13-inch rectangular
2 tsp baking powder	pan. Bake for 40 minutes, or until tester inserted
1 tsp salt	in center comes out clean. Cool completely on
$\frac{1}{3}$ C buttermilk	wire rack. When cool, cut into serving pieces.
3 C coarsely grated zucchini	
$\frac{1}{2}$ C chopped nuts	**8 servings**

DECORATING HATS

do you play as hard as you work? If not, make a date with your funny-bone, because giggles are good for you, body and soul. Charades and scavenger hunts are fun, but you're never to old to play dress-up. Remember, "Fools may invent fashions wise men (and women) will wear." Scour closets and discount stores for hats — derbies, fedoras, berets, boaters, baseball/ski caps, tiaras — one per guest. Arrange scissors, stapler, pens, and glue gun on a table along with bits and bobs — buttons, lace, ribbon, sequins, feathers, tulle, costume jewelry, artificial flowers and fruit — to rejuvenate the hats. Offer to photograph each guest in her new chapeau.

tea seems to have tickled one funnybone: "Tea is an affront to luncheon and an insult to dinner."

— Mark Twain

"WASH THE DISHES, WIPE THE DISHES, RING THE BELL FOR TEA;
THREE GOOD WISHES, THREE GOOD KISSES I WILL GIVE TO THEE."

— *nursery rhyme*

may

MOTHER GOOSE NURSERY TEA

mother Goose Day was created to share the delights of traditional nursery rhymes with a new generation. No one knows if there was a real Mother Goose, but she might have been the Emperor Charlemagne's mother, who was affectionately called Goose-Footed Bertha. A French book published in 1650 refers to a tale that is "like a Mother Goose story," or old wives' tale, and in 1697 Charles Perrault published a collection of fairy tales entitled *Stories of My Mother Goose*. Translated into English, *Cinderella, Little Red Riding Hood,* and *Sleeping Beauty* became part of our childhood.

Legend persists that Bostonian Elizabeth Vergoose was the real Mother Goose. Her son-in-law supposedly published, in 1719, the rhymes and songs she sang to lull her grandchildren to sleep. But no copy of *Songs for the Nursery, or Mother Goose Melodies* has ever been found.

Jack be nimble, Jill be quick
Jump on over to 83 Partridge Lane
for Mother Goose's Nursery tea.
Bring your favorite doll or stuffed animal.
Sunday, May 5

during the Victorian and Edwardian eras, children took their tea in the nursery with their nanny. Simple, filling food and a plain cake were served with cambric tea — black tea laced with lots of milk and sugar. The children were taught, first and foremost, to mind their manners.

Beverages
Caffeine-free Children's Tea
or Cambric tea

Ginger peach tea for adults

Strawberry lemonade

Savories
Ants on a log — celery sticks
filled with peanut butter and
dotted with raisins

Miniature ham 'n' cheese
scones

Sandwiches
Pooh's banana-honey on
whole-wheat bread

Humpty Dumpty Egg-and-
Almond Sandwiches (see recipe)

Sweets
Peter Rabbit carrot cupcakes
with cream cheese icing

Fruit kabobs

Goose-shaped sugar cookies

SETTING THE SCENE

Create a clutch of golden "goose" eggs. Prick raw eggs top and bottom with a needle and carefully blow out the contents. Dye the eggs bright yellow, and thread dry shells on narrow pastel ribbons. Knot ribbons at each end and staple-gun the long ends at different heights high inside a window frame.

For a centerpiece, purchase a plastic/plaster/papier-mâché goose from a garden-supply or crafts shop. Fashion a big pastel-colored bow for the goose's neck and tuck fresh blossoms in the knot. If you're feeling crafty, make Mother Goose a scarf or hat (try a doll's bonnet stuffed with tissue) and a pair of tiny wire spectacles. Elevate your creation on a footed cake plate and ring with a colorful circle of potted primroses.

For music, most kids love to sing, especially rounds and silly songs. If you don't have a piano or can't play the guitar, check the family-favorites and folk-song sections at the music store for sing-along tapes.

HUMPTY DUMPTY EGG-AND-ALMOND SANDWICHES

6 hard-boiled eggs, chopped finely	Mix together all ingredients. Spread on oatmeal bread and serve.
$\frac{1}{2}$ C blanched almonds, chopped finely	
3 Tbsp champagne mustard	
$\frac{1}{4}$ C scallions, minced	
$\frac{1}{2}$ C mayonnaise	
Salt and pepper to taste	

2 cups egg salad

the motto of this sweet celebration is "Either alone or in sharing, read childhood nursery favorites and feel the warmth of Mother Goose's embrace." In addition to reading, you could play games inspired by nursery rhymes. Remember Ring around the Rosie, London Bridge Is Falling Down, A Tisket a Tasket, and Duck, Duck Goose?

Take a cue from this rhyme: "Cackle, cackle, Mother Goose, / Have you any feathers loose? / Truly have I pretty fellow / Quite enough to fill a pillow." Cut "feathers" from construction paper and place them in a pillowcase. Give each child a pillowcase with which to catch the feathers you'll toss from your pillowcase.

You might also tell the story of *The Goose That Laid the Golden Egg* and hold a hunt for an egg dyed bright yellow. A book such as *Miss Spider's Tea Party,* by David Kirk, would make a grand prize.

the maiden who,

On the first of May,

Goes to the fields

At the break of day,

And washes in dew

From the hawthorn tree

Shall ever afterwards

Beautiful be.

— old English rhyme

june

MIDSUMMER CELEBRATION TEA

the summer solstice marks the day when the sun appears to reach its zenith and stand still in the sky. In the northern hemisphere the longest day and shortest night fall between June 21 and June 24. All through the ages people have celebrated Midsummer Day with fire festivals to honor the sun. Festivities would begin on Midsummer Eve, and, in many places, merrymakers built blazing bonfires and "hand in hand, with fairy grace" sang and danced the night away. Lovers jumped over flickering flames, two by two, to bring long life and good luck to their union.

Pagans gathered flowers and herbs on this mystical night to weave magical spells. Flaming wreaths were cast into rivers. Blossoms and grain were tossed into bonfires to secure the sun's blessing on the crops. You might like to celebrate the solstice with an outdoor twilight tea.

Come celebrate Midsummer Eve
Hand-in-hand, with fairy grace, at a Twilight Tea
Saturday, June 23

a small yellow flower, Saint-John's-Wort (an herb) was believed to be especially effective at warding off evil spirits. Hung from windows and doorways, it supposedly protected the household from lightning and madness. But as Shakespeare knew, a little madness on a midsummer night could be great fun.

Beverages
Iced Rose Petal Tea (see recipe)

White wine

Savories
Individual herb quiches

Marinated lentil salad

Sandwiches
Smoked ham and English mustard, on sourdough bread

Dilled shrimp salad, on white bread

Nasturtium butter, on whole-wheat bread

Sweets
Apple-nut muffins

Whole strawberries dipped in sour cream and brown sugar

Chocolate biscotti

Coconut macaroons

SETTING THE SCENE

the great outdoors is calling. If you don't have a backyard, head to a public park. Prop large colorful pillows against tree trunks and hang wind socks or beribboned banners in the branches. Scatter pillows and spread sheets on the grass. If there is no table, arrange the food picnic-style on a sheet. (It will look more appealing if you can vary the height with a footed cake stand or tiered server.)

For a centerpiece, cluster dozens of votive candles (in glass holders) in concentric circles on the ground if you can't have a bonfire. Invite departing guests to take a candle from the communal fire to recall the sun's warmth.

For music, Mendelssohn's *Overture to a Midsummer Night's Dream,* of course, but Elizabethan madrigals (check the classical music section) or dulcimer music would be equally evocative.

ICED ROSE PETAL TEA
by Bertha Reppert, from Herb Teas for Pleasure *(©Rosemary House, Inc.)*

4 C boiling water	Steep ingredients, then strain. Store in the refrigerator for several days to let flavors develop.
1 C red rose petals	
1 tea bag	

8 servings

WEAVING THE MAYPOLE

Invite guests to help create a Maypole, an old symbol of fertility and good fortune. In the ground plant a broomstick or tall pole from the lumberyard (our ancestors would have used a hawthorn sapling). Attach an even number of fluttering, rainbow-colored ribbons (longer than the pole) to the top and crown it with painted eggs, flowers, or balloons. Then toast each other with a glass of wine, and, grasping a ribbon, dance around the pole weaving the ribbon up and down, imitating the rising and setting of the sun.

In addition to nasturtiums and roses, many other flowers are edible — pansies, lilacs, johnny-jump-ups, violets, daylilies, carnations, calendulas, and scented geraniums, for example. Make sure they are pesticide-free, or purchase flowers raised commercially for food. Look for them at upscale grocers and health food stores.

LADY LIBERTY TEA

Pax, the goddess of peace, was honored in Roman times with feasting and revelry on July fourth. Perhaps she inspired sculptor F.A. Bartholdi's colossal statue *Liberty Enlightening the World,* which the French government presented to our nation on July 4, 1884, in commemoration of the French and American Revolutions.

Our revolution began on the night of December 16, 1773. Boston Harbor became a teapot when the Sons of Liberty infused 342 crates of "that pestilent British herb" with icy salt water to make "...a cup of tea for the fishes."

Tea parties were a popular form of entertainment in the American colonies. Many households possessed elegant teaware, but tea was boycotted when patriots united to protest the tyranny of "taxation without representation." The Daughters of Liberty supported the boycott by brewing "Liberty Tea," made with bark, berries, leaves, or herbs.

You might like to salute the birth of the revolution with a Lady Liberty Tea.

A party without representation by you is tyranny!
Join me for a Lady Liberty Tea
Saturday, July 4th

the Daughters of Liberty supported the boycott of British tea. One patriot hosted a party to formally bid adieu to her treasured teaware:

A Lady's Adieu to Her Tea-Table

FAREWELL the Tea-board with your gaudy attire,
Ye cups and ye saucers that I did admire;
To my cream pot and tongs I now bid adieu;
That pleasure's all fled that I once found in you.
. . . No more shall my teapot so generous be
In filling the cups with this pernicious tea,
For I'll fill it with water and drink out the same,
Before I lose Liberty that dearest name. . .

This patriotic menu includes Boston beaners — cold baked beans on Boston brown bread.

Beverages
Ceylon iced tea with crystallized mint leaves

Lemonade shandy

Savories
Multicolored Coleslaw with Fresh Caraway (see recipe)

Watermelon pickles

Sandwiches
Smoked turkey with chutney, on cracked wheat bread

Open-faced mozzarella cheese with sun-dried tomato and fresh basil

Boston beaners

Sweets
Blueberry muffins

Raspberry thumbprint cookies

Chocolate chip–pecan cookies

Coconut cake with a Lady Liberty statuette in the center, ringed with sparklers to be lit at dusk

SETTING THE SCENE

Celebrating the glorious Fourth indoors is unimaginable, but it's likely to be hotter than a firecracker outside, so head for shade. Using fishing line, suspend big red, white, and blue cardboard stars (available from party/stationery stores) at different heights from tree branches. Fly the flag! Cover the picnic table with a patchwork quilt or drape with tri-colored bunting (available at craft stores). Use a plastic-lined wheelbarrow or kid's red wagon to house cold drinks.

For a centerpiece, arrange wildflowers in a star-spangled watering can or cluster red, silver, and blue Christmas balls in a striped bowl and tuck tiny paper flags in the gaps.

For music, play Sousa marches, anything by George M. Cohen, and sing-along favorites such as "Yankee Doodle," "America the Beautiful," and "This Land Is Your Land."

MULTICOLORED COLESLAW WITH FRESH CARAWAY

½ lb red cabbage, coarsely shredded	In a large bowl, combine all ingredients and toss thoroughly. Cover and refrigerate for at least 8 hours before serving.
½ lb green cabbage, coarsely shredded	
⅓ lb carrots, shredded	
¼ C fresh caraway leaves, minced	
¼ C cider vinegar	
2 Tbsp canola oil	
1 Tbsp fresh gingerroot, grated	
½ tsp salt	
½ tsp ground black pepper	
	6 servings

to play Tempest in a Teapot, you'll need a child's plastic wading pool, a teapot, and a box of teabags (which were invented by American tea merchant Thomas Sullivan in 1904). Fill the wading pool with water and place a teapot — minus the lid — in the pool's center. Hand each guest three tea bags, and award a Lady Liberty foam crown to the person who lands the most bags in the pot. Those which fall in "Boston Harbor" are out-of-bounds.

Place sheets of newsprint (from an art-supply store), crayons, and markers on a picnic table. Invite guests to create a flag symbolic of their state of mind. Those who are really inspired may include a state motto, flower, and bird or animal. Award a prize to the person who can identify the thirteen original colonies and another to the well-informed individual who can name all fifty states *and* their capitals. Play Uncle Sam Says: It's just like Simon Says, only more patriotic.

a tourist visiting eighteenth-century Boston observed "the ladies here visit, drink tea and indulge in every little piece of gentility to the height of the mode and neglect the affairs of their families with as good grace as the finest ladies in London."

"MAD DOGS AND ENGLISHMEN GO OUT IN THE MIDDAY SUN."

— *Noël Coward*

august

DOG DAYS PICNIC TEA

augustus Caesar thought August a lucky month, and named it after himself when he revised the Roman calendar. There are many opportunities to celebrate this month. August 13 is International Left-Handers Day. The first book ever printed, *The Book of Psalms*, was printed August 14, 1457. National Aviation Day is August 19, the birthday of Orville Wright.

But it's too darn hot! The Dog Days have us in their grip; Sirius, the Dog Star, bigger, brighter, and hotter than the sun, rises early in the morning this time of year. The Romans believed that Sirius, whose name means "scorching," added its heat to the sun. The Egyptians, who venerated the star as a god, credited Sirius with the annual flooding of the Nile River and declared the day a holiday. Plan a long, leisurely afternoon at the beach watching the tide go out, or decamp to a swimming pool.

"Mad dogs and Englishmen go out
in the midday sun,"
so please join me, at three, for a lazy afternoon
sipping tea by the sea.
Friday, August 8

according to *Picnic!* by Edith Stovel, picnics were originally communal meals to which each person contributed a little something. In the nineteenth century, the English developed a Picnic Society, which added entertainment and theatrics to the elegant edibles.

Beverages

Iced teas: a cooling green tea such as Dragon Well or Dimbula black tea

Tropical Cooler with Pineapple Sage and Mint (see recipe)

Savories

Cheddar cheese corn muffins

Assorted ripe olives and cherry tomatoes dipped in vodka and kosher salt

Sandwiches

Watercress, walnuts, and cream cheese on pumpernickel

Tuna salad with apple, on date-nut bread

Sweet Vidalia onion on buttered white bread

Sweets

Lemon-poppy seed loaf

Dog-shaped gingerbread cookies

Peanut butter cookies

SETTING THE SCENE

Mother Nature can't be beat, so you'll just need to define your space. If you have a tent, erect it on the beach. If not, create shade with multiple umbrellas or tether colorful sheets to four poles staked in the sand. Flutter banners, bright ribbons, or wind socks from the poles. Spread a comforter, and add pillows for lounging. Round up and rinse assorted soda and juice bottles. Bury them in sand up to their mouths to outline the perimeter of your comforter. Add some water, and tuck a large sunflower in each bottle to create a flowery border. Give one to each departing guest.

 For music, the sound of the waves gently lapping the shore should be enough, but there's always Handel's "Water Music," James Galway's *Song of the Seashore and Other Melodies of Japan,* or the Beach Boys!

TROPICAL COOLER WITH PINEAPPLE SAGE AND MINT

1½ C water	Bring water to a boil and pour over the pineapple sage and mint leaves and the fresh ginger in a heat-proof bowl. Steep for 15 minutes.
¼ C fresh pineapple sage leaves	
¼ C fresh mint leaves	Strain and discard the herbs. In a pitcher, combine herb liquid with pineapple, papaya, orange, and lime juices. Chill overnight. Just before pouring into a thermos, add sparkling water.
1 Tbsp fresh ginger, minced	
2 C pineapple juice, chilled	
1½ C papaya nectar, chilled	
1 C orange juice, chilled	
¼ C lime juice	
1 qt sparkling mineral water	**2½ quarts**

GOING FISHING

Wrap a cardboard box with fish-patterned paper, leaving the top open. Using a thick stick or wooden dowel and string, craft a "fishing pole." Attach a small magnet (available at hobby/craft shops) to the string. Collect a cache of inexpensive tissue-wrapped gifts with a water theme — miniature shell-shaped soap, travel-sized tubes of bath gel, for example — and label each one with a number. Cut fish from construction paper and poke an open bobby pin through the "mouth." Write a number corresponding to a gift on the back of each fish. Let guests take turns landing a "fish." Award the prize that matches the fish's number.

Invite your guests to create a group sand sculpture. Decorate the creation with seaweed, shells, driftwood, and beach glass.

for a perfect picnic: Prepare iced tea ahead of time; if it turns cloudy, add a splash of boiling water. Freeze tea in a plastic container or rinsed plastic milk carton; remember to leave room at the top for it to expand. Use the container or carton as an icepack to chill food until you're ready to eat.

september

LITERARY TEA

September, rather than January, always seems like the real beginning of the year. The long, lazy summer afternoons are officially over. People walk now with a more purposeful step. There's an undercurrent of excitement in the air. Street fairs and block parties percolate as folks welcome each other back from vacation. And school starts.

September is National Children's Book Month. Perhaps September was honored because so many authors were born in that month: Edgar Rice Burroughs, creator of *Tarzan;* James Fenimore Cooper, *The Last of the Mohicans;* H.G. Wells, *The Time Machine;* James Hilton, *Lost Horizon;* short-story writer O. Henry; and the Greek dramatist Euripedes.

Why not rekindle the love of learning with a literary tea? Many groups of people who love to read and love to talk gather once a month to share a meal, discuss a book, and catch up with each other's lives.

Join me for a novel experience!
Please read The Grass Harp by Truman Capote
and come share your thoughts at a literary tea.
Wednesday, September 16

Samuel Johnson, the man who penned the first English-language dictionary, described himself as "a hardened and shameless tea drinker . . . who with tea amused the evening, with tea solaced the midnight, and with tea welcomed the morning."

MENU

Arrange the food as a buffet on a sideboard or table so that guests may help themselves — freeing you to conduct the discussion.

Beverages
Kenya and Jasmine teas

Savories
Mushroom and onion tartlets

Sandwiches
Curried chicken salad with almonds on multigrain bread

Hummus (see recipe)

Cream cheese, chopped dried apricots and figs on Boston brown bread

Sweets
Madeleines

Chocolate apple cake

Currant tea cakes

SETTING THE SCENE

ⓐ living room, book-lined study, or library with comfortable seating is the ideal setting for your literary tea.

For a centerpiece: In the eighteenth century, bookish society ladies who attempted to replace card parties with more intellectual entertainments were called bluestockings. The name came from the unfashionable blue worsted stockings that ordinary people wore. Create a centerpiece by spray-painting an old boot or high-topped sneaker a deep blue and fill it with asters, September's flower. Display your centerpiece on a stack of books.

For music, classical music, mellow jazz, or New Age instrumentals will sound the right note. Vocals are too distracting, but *Harpestry, A Contemporary Collection* and Wynton Marsalis's *In Gabriel's Garden* are lovely.

HUMMUS
Adapted from Wings of Life Vegetarian Cookery, *by Julie Jordan (Crossing Press)*

2 C canned chickpeas	Mash chickpeas with fork or pulse briefly in food processor. Mix garlic and salt in separate bowl; stir in tahini.
4 cloves garlic, mashed	With wooden spoon, beat in lemon juice. Add a little chickpea liquid or water and beat until sauce has the
1 tsp sea salt	consistency of thick mayonnaise. Beat tahini, garlic, and
½ C tahini	salt into the chickpeas. Add a little at a time, beating
Juice of 1 lemon	until smooth. If mixture is too thick, beat in a little more
2–6 Tbsp chickpea liquid or water	liquid until spreadable. Add fresh parsley. Add salt, if needed.
½ C finely chopped parsley	Cut off the top third and fill miniature pita pockets with hummus.

2 cups

DISCUSSING THE LITERATURE

the activity for this party is discussing the book guests have read. As the host you should prepare several leading questions ahead of time to get the conversational ball rolling. Questions might include: "How did you like the book? What did you like about it?" "Is there anyone who didn't like the book? Why?" "Why do you suppose so-and-so did thus and such?" "Why do you think the author told us blank, but left blank to our imagination?"

Ask questions one at a time and go around the room for each question, inviting guests to share their thoughts. People might choose to answer some questions but skip others. Consult a reading group handbook for more suggestions about leading a discussion. Be sure to ask your guests if they would like to make a reading group a regularly scheduled activity: You might be pleasantly surprised!

according to Rachel Jacobsohn, author of *The Reading Group Handbook*, American book groups have flourished since the early nineteenth century, when New England women met to discuss "serious poetry, non-fiction and publications of the day."

"BRIGHT YELLOW, RED, AND ORANGE / THE LEAVES COME DOWN IN HOSTS/
THE TREES ARE INDIAN PRINCES / BUT SOON THEY'LL TURN TO GHOSTS . . ."
— *William Allingham*

october

HALLOWEEN HIGH TEA

When October gives a party she goes all out — air sweet and crisp as cider, trees trimmed with dancing leaves, and, at the very end, Halloween, a night of mischief and merriment. Our playful holiday has its roots in the Druids' New Year's Eve, Samhain, which was celebrated on October 31. On this, the most magical night of the year, spirits of the dead would cross over to partake in the harvest festivities or warm themselves at their former hearths. Since no one could predict if a good or evil spirit would come home, people disguised themselves to trick malevolent ghosts. Children today who eagerly ask each other "What are you going to be for Halloween?" carry on this tradition.

Over time, Samhain rites were combined with a Christian holy day, All Hallow's Eve, which was eventually transformed into the secular holiday Halloween. How about celebrating with a high tea while greeting trick-or-treaters?

There's a party brewing at 7 Maple Road.
On Halloween, don't tempt fate; join me at eight
or the goblins'll get you!

Irish tales tell of Jack, a miserly drunkard, banned from heaven and also barred from hell because of a nasty trick he had once played on the devil. Condemned to wander the earth for eternity, Jack snatched a coal from Satan and thrust it in a turnip lantern to light his solitary way. Centuries later, the original hollow turnip was upgraded to a pumpkin, our grinning jack-o'-lantern.

SETTING THE SCENE

decorations should be abundant, recalling the harvest. Collect masses of colored leaves and bittersweet vine and twist them into wreaths and garlands. Wire on apples and nuts and tuck in brilliant cockscomb and marigold flowers. Scatter marigold petals to mark a path from doorway to table as they do in Mexico, where families construct an altar decorated with candles and personal mementos to honor their dead.

For a centerpiece, suspend a teapot or a teakettle (secure the lid to spout and handle with fishing line) over your serving table. Thread a large rubber spider or bat and a handful of fake cobweb (from a craft or party store) on a long piece of fishing line and tie the other end of the line to a toothpick. Poke the toothpick through the spout and position it crosswise over the base of the spout on the inside of the pot. Create a large orange and black bow for the pot handle.

For music, "The Sorcerer's Apprentice," "Danse Macabre," and "Nocturnes" by Sibelius or Chopin have spooktacular appeal.

SPICY MUSTARD SPREAD

8 Tbsp butter, softened	Using an electric mixer or a food processor, cream together all ingredients.
1 Tbsp finely chopped fresh parsley	Spread on bread or crackers.
1 Tbsp finely chopped fresh basil	
1 Tbsp spicy mustard	

About ½ cup

TELLING FORTUNES

fortune-telling games have been played on Halloween since time immemorial. Give each guest a chestnut to toss into the fireplace or on a grill. If it burns brightly, the thrower will thrive. Should the flame flicker, anticipate a passionate lover. If the nut hisses, the owner has a terrible temper; should it burst open, a quarrel will ensue.

Place two brooms on the floor to form an X. Invite each guest to turn around three times and toss a horseshoe over his or her left shoulder. If it lands face up, expect good fortune from the direction in which the shoe landed. If the shoe lands face down, watch out!

bake a ginger spice cake with charms inside. Individually wrap a ring, coin, thimble, button, and other charms in pieces of waxed paper. (Old charm bracelets, earrings, and novelty stores are good sources.) The person who finds a coin in his or her slice of cake can anticipate wealth. A wishbone grants wishes, a heart promises your heart's desire, and a ring signifies marriage. A key symbolizes success, a button indicates a bachelor, and a thimble predicts a spinster.

november

VICTORIAN AFTERNOON TEA

November is British Appreciation Month and afternoon tea is the quintessential British experience. Teatime became a national obsession during the Victorian era. Alexandria Victoria, Queen of the United Kingdom of Great Britain and Ireland and Empress of India, reigned for sixty-three years. Some contend that her first command was "Bring me a cup of tea and the Times." During her rule the British began to cultivate tea in India, so drinking black tea became a patriotic as well as a pleasurable act. Introduced to the custom of afternoon tea by one of her ladies-in-waiting, Queen Victoria, who delighted in ceremony and tradition, frequently took tea with her husband, Prince Albert, and their nine children.

Who doesn't long for a return to romance and civility, and an age when time seemed to move more slowly? Before the holiday season begins in earnest, set aside time to celebrate British Appreciation Month with a Victorian afternoon tea.

If you would merry be, join me for the festival of afternoon tea!
Saturday, November 11, 3–5 PM

"afternoon tea is probably the simplest fashion in which to exercise hospitality. Pretty cups and saucers are among the possessions of which the young house-keeper has a generous store and they will make an attractive array on her afternoon tea table."
— Catherine Terhune Herrick

Beverages

Assam or Darjeeling tea

Sherry

Savories

Curried almonds

Sandwiches

Watercress and Stilton
Sandwiches (see recipe)

Rare roast beef with
horseradish mayonnaise on
whole-wheat bread

Cucumber and sweet butter
on white bread

Sweets

Lemon scones with lemon curd
and clotted cream

Trifle or
Victoria sponge cake

Petits Fours

SETTING THE SCENE

get out your laciest linens; your etched, pressed, or cut-glass accessories; and gleaming silvery serving pieces. Layer a small cloth or pretty shawl over a floor-length tablecloth for added drama. Line trays and cake plates with doilies or dainty napkins. Make a lush bow with wired ribbon for tray handles and tiered servers; garnish platters with beribboned bundles of fresh blossoms and sweet-smelling herbs.

For a centerpiece, collect a small, a medium, and a large lidded hatbox from a secondhand, craft, or decorative-accessory store. Stack the medium box on top of the large one and top with a framed photo of Queen Victoria or a collection of vintage family photos in decorative frames. Position the small box next to the large one. Prop a beribboned parasol and a pretty hat next to the stacked boxes and drape a pair of gloves and a fan over the small box.

For music, piano selections are traditionally played at teatime. Pieces by Liszt, Schubert, or Mendelssohn would be appropriate, as would something more contemporary — Jim Gibson's *The Art of Tea*, for instance.

WATERCRESS AND STILTON SANDWICHES

2 oz Stilton cheese or $\frac{1}{4}$ C crumbled blue cheese, at room temperature 2 Tbsp dry port wine 2 Tbsp low-fat or nonfat sour cream 2 oz low-fat cream cheese 8 slices thin white or wheat bread, toasted Ground black pepper $1\frac{1}{2}$ C minced watercress or garden cress	Using an electric mixer, cream the Stilton or blue cheese, port, sour cream, and cream cheese. Spread the mixture on four slices of the bread and sprinkle with black pepper. Scatter on the cress, then top with the other four pieces of toast. Cut out small shapes with a cookie cutter, or trim the crusts and cut diagonally into halves, then halve again. **4 servings**

MAKING LAVENDER SACHETS

Victorian women prided themselves on their needlework skills. Linen closets and lingerie drawers were freshened with sweet-smelling herbal sachets sewn from decorative fabric scraps. Even if you and your guests don't have time to sew, you can still make a lavender sachet to scent and protect your linens. Shop flea markets and secondhand clothing stores for inexpensive vintage fabric gloves. About a month before the party, visit a store that sells herbs, spices, and oils and assemble the following recipe. On the day of the party, arrange the assorted gloves and bowl of premade sachet on a table along with embroidery needles and thread, and narrow silk ribbon. Invite guests to fill gloves to within 2 inches of the top and close with a running stitch. Trim with a silk bow.

FOREVER LAVENDER SACHET

16 oz   lavender flowers
2 oz   sweet woodruff
½ oz   oak moss
½ oz   thyme
8 oz   dried orange peel

4 oz   benzoin
Several handfuls of other herbs and
   flowers (such as peppermint,
   violets, and rose geranium petals)
¼ oz   mixture of cloves and anise

Combine all of the ingredients and shake occasionally during several weeks of aging.

the royal family's activities were a model for the nation, and soon society ladies were presiding over elaborate tea tables and serving toast "as thin as poppy leaves" to their friends at four o'clock in the afternoon. Primers explained exactly how every detail from apparel (an extravagant hat, white kid gloves, and parasol were de rigueur) to etiquette should be achieved. A gracious hostess should never ask, "Would you like another cup?" Rather, she must refill guests' cups until they indicate that they have had enough.

"WHEN I HAVE A HOME, AND CAN DO AS I WILL / DECEMBER MAY RAGE OVER OCEAN AND HILL/
AND BATTER MY DOOR — AS HE DOES ONCE A YEAR / I LAUGH AT HIS STORMING, AND DRINK HIS GOOD CHEER."

— *old English song*

december

ST. NICHOLAS BRUNCH TEA

the original St. Nicholas was a fourth-century Turkish bishop, the patron saint of brides and children. Legend tells of the time the compassionate man learned of three sisters unable to marry because their parents were too poor to provide them a dowry. At night, so no one would know of his generosity, St. Nicholas visited their house and tossed a handful of gold coins through an open window. The coins fell into stockings the girls had hung by the fire to dry, and now the sisters could be wed. Dutch settlers carried with them to the New World their custom of filling children's stockings with gifts and pretending they were from St. Nicholas.

A delightful change from a caroling or tree trimming cocktail party is a St. Nicholas brunch tea. Invite guests to bring an unwrapped gift for someone less fortunate, and you provide the wrappings. Contact a local shelter, nursing home, or hospital to ask what kinds of donations are most needed.

Please join me for the cup that cheers and make the season bright by bringing an unwrapped gift for someone very young or very old. P.S. If you've done your Christmas shopping early, you clever thing, bring those presents along for a wrapping party.

Saturday, December 6, 11 AM—1 PM

In Holland presents are brought by St. Nicholas on December sixth. Fondly called Sinterklaas, the regal bishop travels from Spain on a white horse. On St. Nicholas Eve children place their shoes by the fire and stuff them with hay as fodder for the saint's snowy steed. In the morning good children are rewarded with sweets, but rude or lazy youngsters find a birch rod placed next to their shoes as a warning.

Beverages
English breakfast tea

Hot Dutch chocolate

Savories
Mushroom quiche

Grilled Tomatoes with Herbed Cheese (see recipe)

Sausage

Sweets
Oatmeal muffins with marmalade

Oliebollen (Dutch raisin-studded doughnuts)

Individual mince pies

Sugar cookie cutouts in Christmas-y shapes

SETTING THE SCENE

Some people put up their Christmas decorations the day after Thanksgiving, which seems to rush the season. Try decorating in stages, aiming to finish up by Christmas Eve. As the song says, we've got twelve days to celebrate between December 25 and January 6. Like the Dutch, you could amass bowls of blooming bulbs, such as narcissus, for early December decorations. If their scent is too sweet for you, how about gaily wrapped pots of rosemary, bay, or other green herbs?

 For a centerpiece made in the wink of an eye, load a child's chair, toy sled, wagon, or truck with stuffed animals and dolls, wooden toys, and shiny red apples.

 For music, use Christmas carols, of course! Liona Boyd's *A Guitar for Christmas, Carols from Clare,* with its collection of traditional and lesser known English, Polish, French, Czech, and Basque tunes and the Chieftains' *The Bells of Dublin* are favorites.

GRILLED TOMATOES WITH HERBED CHEESE

Ingredients	Instructions
8 oz fresh goat cheese	By hand or in a food processor, combine goat cheese, garlic, and basil until well blended. If cheese is too thick, add a bit of cream or milk. Store in an airtight container in the refrigerator, allowing flavors to blend for at least a day. Fill tomatoes with cheese mixture and grill until cheese melts.
1 garlic clove, minced	
¼ C minced fresh basil leaves	
4 fresh tomatoes, halved with insides scooped out	

8 servings tomatoes, 1 cup cheese

the Hallmark company estimates that most folks wrap thirty gifts each holiday. It's more fun to wrap up this chore in the company of friends. Set up a wrapping center on a sturdy table or counter with paper, tissue paper, ribbon, yarn, raffia, stickers, scissors, tape, and glue sticks. For those who'd like to create their own wrapping paper, provide brown butcher paper, poster paints, brushes, Christmas cookie cutters (to trace around), rubber stamps, ink pads, and glitter. Gift tags may be made from old greeting cards. A paper towel/foil tube is a good "box" for scarves, gloves, or small toys. Simply wrap the tube with tissue paper, leaving an extra 2 to 3 inches at either end. Gently gather the paper at each end and tie with a bow close to the tube.

Another fun activity is to fill a stocking with small unwrapped household objects — lemon reamer, thimble, paper clip, for example. Guests dip a hand in Santa's stocking and, without looking, try to identify the mystery object.

Maps, posters, sheet music, wallpaper, foreign newspapers, and the funnies are interesting alternatives to traditional Christmas wrap.

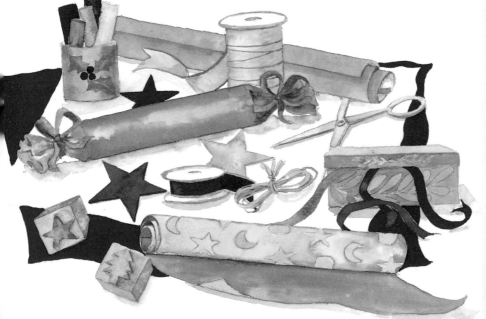

MENU

*Simply provide beverages,
savories, and sweets — your
guests will bring the main dishes.*

WINTER SOLSTICE TEA

In northern climates the days get colder and shorter until about December 22, the winter solstice, when the sun seems to be swallowed by the dark. Long before there was a Christmas, people gathered in late December to kindle the "fire of hospitality" and drive away the dark. Druids decorated oak trees with gilded apples and lighted candles to honor their sun god, Balder. Mistletoe and holly, sacred because they mysteriously bear berries in the dead of winter, were ceremonially harvested and hung indoors. The Romans trimmed trees with trinkets and candles and exchanged holly wreaths during their rowdy Saturnalia feast. The Christian church adapted the long tradition of midwinter festivities when it designated Christmas as the birthday of the "Light of the World." So if Santa is not your cup of tea, ask guests to bring a traditional holiday dish to a Winter Solstice Tea.

HOT MULLED CRANBERRY AND BOURBON PUNCH

2 C cranberry juice	Combine cranberry juice, Earl Grey tea, cinnamon sticks, and a few whole cloves in a nonstick pan. Sweeten to taste with brown sugar and heat gently until just boiling. Remove from heat, add ½ cup bourbon (if desired), and ladle into cups.
2 C Earl Grey tea	
2 cinnamon sticks, broken	
A few whole cloves	
Brown sugar to taste	
½ C bourbon (optional)	**8 servings**

SETTING THE SCENE

Wire a swag of mixed evergreens, ivy, pepper berries, and mistletoe to your door, or frame the door and windows with greenery, to celebrate life in the dead of winter. Fill bowls or baskets with clove-studded orange pomanders.

For a centerpiece, arrange pine boughs, fresh eucalyptus, curly willow branches, star-of-Bethlehem, and pinecones in a tall container. Hang snowflake ornaments, matte silver and frosted balls, glass icicles, and dried orange slices (sun symbols) from the boughs.

For music, Windham Hill Artists' "A Winter's Solstice" series, George Winston's *December,* and the Revels' *To Drive the Dark Away: Songs and Dances for the Winter Solstice* are interesting options.

BURNING THE YULE LOG

Long ago a large log — found or donated, but never bought — was ceremoniously dragged into the house at this time of the year. Folks believed that as the log burned, bad luck and old grievances went up in smoke. Revelers paid tribute to the Yule log with special songs and dances. At the end of the festivities a piece of the charred log was carefully saved to light next year's log. The ashes were solemnly sprinkled on doorways and around trees to secure blessings for hearth and home.

Invite guests to celebrate the solstice by writing their wishes or grievances on pieces of wood and tossing them into a communal fire. Hand out candles for a torchlight procession around the blazing bonfire. Also provide a basket of evergreens. Guests who'd like to dream of a future love should place an evergreen sprig under their pillows this night.

"life is a
cup to be
filled, not
drained."

—Anonymous

Country Tea Parties, by Maggie Stuckey. 64 pages. Cloth. ISBN 0-88266-935-4.

Hardie Newton's Celebration of Flowers, by Hardie Newton. 192 pages. Cloth. ISBN 0-88266-997-4.

The Herbal Palate Cookbook: Delicious Recipes That Showcase the Versatility and Magic of Fresh Herbs, by Maggie Oster and Sal Gilbertie. 176 pages. Paperback. ISBN 1-58017-025-0.

Herbal Sweets, by Ruth Bass. 64 pages. Cloth. ISBN 0-88266-922-2.

The Herbal Tea Garden: Planning, Planting, Harvesting & Brewing, by Marietta Marshall Marcin. 224 pages. Paperback. ISBN 0-88266-827-7.

Keeping Entertaining Simple, by Martha Storey. 160 pages. Paperback. ISBN 1-58017-056-0.

Nature Printing with Herbs, Fruits & Flowers, by Laura Donnelly Bethmann. 96 pages. Cloth. ISBN 0-88266-929-X.

Picnic! Recipes and Menus for Outdoor Enjoyment, by Edith Stovel. 176 pages. Paperback. ISBN 0-88266-586-3.

Weekend! A Menu Cookbook for Relaxed Entertaining, by Edith Stovel. 176 pages. Paperback. ISBN 0-88266-847-1.

These books and other Storey books are available at your bookstore, farm store, garden center, or directly from Storey Books, Schoolhouse Road, Pownal, Vermont 05261, or by calling 1-800-441-5700. www.storey.com